AMERICAN HUMANE

Protecting Children & Animals Since 1877

Top 10 Small Mammals for Kids

Ann Graham Gaines

Enslow Elementary

an imprint of

Enslow Publishers, Inc.

40 Industrial Road
Box 398
Berkeley Heights, NJ 07922
USA

http://www.enslow.com

AMERICAN HUMANE

Protecting Children & Animals Since 1877

Founded in 1877, the American Humane Association is the oldest national organization dedicated to protecting both children and animals. Through a network of child and animal protection agencies and individuals, the American Humane Association develops policies, legislation, curricula, and training programs to protect children and animals from abuse, neglect, and exploitation. To learn how you can support the vision of a nation where no child or animal will ever be a victim of willful abuse or neglect, visit www.americanhumane.org, phone (303) 792-9900, or write to the American Humane Association at 63 Inverness Drive East, Englewood, Colorado, 80112-5117.

Enslow Elementary, an imprint of Enslow Publishers, Inc.

Enslow Elementary® is a registered trademark of Enslow Publishers, Inc.

The top 10 small mammals are approved by the American Humane Association and are listed alphabetically.

Library of Congress Cataloging-in-Publication Data
Gaines, Ann.
    Top 10 small mammals for kids / Ann Graham Gaines.
        p. cm. — (Top pets for kids with American Humane)
    Summary: "Provides facts on the top ten small mammals for kids and how to care for them"—Provided by publisher.
    Includes bibliographical references and index.
    ISBN-13: 978-0-7660-3075-6
    ISBN-10: 0-7660-3075-X
    1. Pets—Juvenile literature. 2. Mammals—Juvenile literature.
    I. Title. II. Title: Top ten small mammals for kids.
    SF416.2.G35 2008
    636.9—dc22
                                    2007038480

Printed in the United States of America

10 9 8 7 6 5 4 3 2 1

To Our Readers:
We have done our best to make sure that all Internet Addresses in this book were active and appropriate when we went to press. However, the author and publisher have no control over and assume no liability for the material available on those Internet sites or on other Web sites they may link to. Any comments or suggestions can be sent by e-mail to comments@enslow.com or to the address on the back cover.

♻ Enslow Publishers, Inc., is committed to printing our books on recycled paper. The paper in every book contains 10% to 30% post-consumer waste (PCW). The cover board on the outside of each book contains 100% PCW. Our goal is to do our part to help young people and the environment too!

Cover Photo: Arco Images/Alamy
Interior Photos: Alamy/Arco Images, pp. 1, 8, 14, 15, 32, 40, 41, 48; Alamy/Juniors Bildarchiv, pp. 3, 10, 22, 25, 43; Alamy/Papilio, p. 12; Alamy/Maximilian Weinzierl, pp. 18, 28 right, 36; Alamy/imagebroker, p. 28 left; Alamy/Digital Archive Japan, p. 34; Alamy/Stockbyte, p. 38; Animals Animals–Earth Scenes/Jorg & Petra Wegner, p. 30; iStockphoto.com/ Maartje van Caspel, p. 2; iStockphoto.com/2692032, p. 4; iStockphoto.com/Seb Chandler, pp. 5, 11, 16, 42; iStockphoto.com/ Emilia Stasiak, pp. 9, 37 right; iStockphoto.com/Nikita Buida, p. 17; iStockphoto.com/Eric Isselée, pp. 23, 27, 39; iStockphoto.com/Redphotographer, p. 24; iStockphoto.com/Tuyen Nguyen, p. 26; iStockphoto.com/Matt Staples, p. 31; iStockphoto.com/jkitan, p. 37 left; iStockphoto.com/Maria Bibikova, p. 46; iStockphoto.com/Joshua Blake, p. 47; Photo Edit/Richard Hutchings, p. 7; Photo Edit/Steve Skjold, p. 20; Photo Edit/Nancy Sheehan, p. 21; Photo Edit/Cindy Charles, p. 45.

Contents

A Small, Furry Pet

Are you thinking about getting a pet? How about one that is small and furry? If that sounds perfect, think about getting a small mammal. Small mammals can make excellent pets!

The first thing you need to know, of course, is exactly what a small mammal is. When veterinarians (vets) talk about small

◀ Like most small pet mammals, hamsters are cute, furry, soft, and fun to watch!

mammals as pets, they usually mean gerbils, guinea pigs, hamsters, mice, and rats. Other small pet mammals include the more exotic chinchilla (chin-CHILL-a), degu (DAY-goo), ferret, and hedgehog. Pet rabbits are also thought of as small mammals, even though some grow to be bigger than cats!

Why do people like small mammals as pets? There are many reasons:

1. They are soft and furry.
2. Many of them are cute.
3. They are interesting to watch.
4. They are usually very active. Most race around, burrow, and hide. Some climb. Others seem like chewing machines!
5. They are usually quiet pets.
6. Most do not need much room.
7. Many like to be played with.

Gerbils and other small mammals are usually very active and fun to watch.

How can you find out if a small mammal is the right pet for your family? You need information, of course. There are several ways to get the information:

1. Talk to a vet.
2. Talk to other small mammal owners.
3. Go to the library and look for pet books. A librarian can help you find out about the animal that interests you.

Once you have your facts, talk with your family. Decide together if you can handle the responsibility of owning a small mammal. Be honest. Can you take proper care of this kind of pet? Some small mammals will need special food. All of them need fresh water every day, and their cage cleaned at least once a week. That can be a stinky job! Are you willing to do it?

For some animals, you will be taking on this job for a very long time. Chinchillas can live up to 22 years! Hedgehogs can live up to 10 years. Pet rabbits can live up to 12. If you adopt mice, on the other hand, you will not

▲

Some small mammals live a very long time. Chinchillas can live up to 22 years!

have them nearly as long. They usually live a year and a half or two years.

Next, keep in mind that it could cost a lot to keep a small mammal. It is true that buying one mouse, for example, does not cost very much. But all small mammals need a cage, a special kind of water bottle, special food, exercise equipment, and sometimes even more. Plus, when your pet will have to go to the vet, it can be expensive.

Having any pet is a big responsibility. But if you choose to adopt a small, furry animal as your pet, you will have lots of fun, too!

Healthy and Happy Small Mammals

What does it take to be sure a small mammal stays healthy and happy?

Food and Water

Small mammals do not all eat the same kinds of food. Many eat only plants, but some, including the ferret and the hedgehog, do not eat plants at all.

◄ Degus love to eat fresh, raw vegetables. But veggies are just one part of a degu's diet.

Stores sell special food pellets for different kinds of small mammals. Your pet will also need other food. For guinea pigs and gerbils, this will be vegetables. Rabbits need both vegetables and hay. Also, most small mammals need things to chew, such as tree branches. To find out exactly what your pet will need, read up—and ask your vet!

A sipper bottle is how your pet will get the water it needs. Be sure there is always fresh water to drink.

▼

Like all other animals, small mammals need water. Some cannot drink out of a bowl. Instead, they need a special sipper bottle hung upside-down on the side of their cage.

A Comfortable Home

Small pet mammals usually live in cages with a solid, not wire, bottom. Some can also live in a glass box, called a terrarium (ter-RARE-ee-um). The size of their cage and what they need in it varies from animal to animal. A mouse can live in a small cage. A rat needs a cage that is at least 24 inches wide. Rabbits and ferrets need very large cages, measuring about five feet in length.

Inside their home, all small mammals need three things: bedding, a place to hide, and exercise equipment. The bedding you put down on the bottom should be hay or wood shavings (but not cedar chips, which have oils that can make small mammals sick). To give your pet a place to hide, you might want to put a cardboard tube or box in its cage.

Rabbits and ferrets need to be let out of their cages every day so they can roam

A large home is best for a rabbit. It should have plenty of room to move around, dark places to hide, and soft straw bedding.

▼

▲

Rats and other small mammals need exercise equipment. Tubes, ladders, and platforms are great for climbing.

around. Make sure they are in a safe area where there are no plants or electrical cords. This will keep them from getting sick or hurt. Other small mammals can get their exercise from running through special tubes, or using exercise wheels or balls made especially for these animals.

How to Choose the Pet for You

Chances are if you have looked up pictures of small pet mammals you think they are all cute. So how will you decide which is the pet for you?

If you think you might like a ferret, hedgehog, or degu, the very first thing to do is to find out if it is legal to keep these animals where you live. In some places, lawmakers worry that if ferrets, for example, escape and start living in the wild, they will destroy crops. Ask an adult to call the animal control officer in your town to ask this question.

Next, think hard about why you want a pet, and what you hope having a pet will be like. What interests you? If you would like to be able to watch your pet during the day, a gerbil might be a good choice. They are active during the day. On the other hand, hamsters like to sleep during the day and play at night.

If you would like to have more than one small, furry pet, think about getting degus.

▲

Hedgehogs may be cute, but in some places it is against the law to have them as pets. Have an adult check the laws in your area.

If you want to spend a lot of time watching your pets' activities, gerbils will be a great choice. They are active during the day.

They are actually only happy in a group. Experts sometimes recommend that people get two ferrets, but this can be a lot to handle. Ferrets are very energetic!

Do you want a pet that you can pick up? Mice are not easy to handle. They will try to get out of your hands, and if they escape, they are very hard to find. A chinchilla may take a while to get used to you, but after awhile it will probably come to you to be petted if you can be very quiet and calm.

Although chinchillas rarely bite, they may do so if held too tight. And they have very sharp teeth! Hedgehogs and ferrets have painful bites also. They should be handled very carefully. Gerbils and hamsters are easier to handle.

Think about your home. Is there a room in your house or apartment that can easily be closed off, and where you can let your pet out? If so, a ferret might be perfect for you. If you have a big yard where you can put up a pen, you could get a rabbit. If you have room for only a small cage, mice will be a good choice.

Finally, think about your family. If you have very young brothers or sisters, a chinchilla will not be a good choice. Chinchillas are easily frightened and might get hurt trying to escape from a small child. Experts also say guinea pigs, mice, and hamsters are not very good choices for families with small children, such as preschoolers.

When it comes time to actually get your pet, there are still more choices to make. Many pet stores sell small mammals. You may need to go to a breeder, however,

Hamsters make good classroom pets, too!

▲

Before you buy your pet from a pet store, be sure to check out the store. It is important that all of the animals there look clean, healthy, and well-cared for.

to get one of the more exotic ones, such as a degu or ferret. One excellent place to get a pet is from a rescue group. This is an organization that takes care of animals that have been abandoned or neglected. Never try to get a pet from the wild. If you find an injured rabbit in your yard, for example, do not take it inside. Wild animals never make good pets and should be left in the wild.

Chinchillas can jump very high.

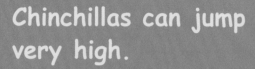

Appearance

- Large in size compared to other rodents, with a body 7 to 10 inches in length
- Long, bushy tail that adds another 5 to 6 inches
- Large ears
- Huge eyes
- Extremely soft fur
- Usually white in color, but can also be cream, brown, or gray-blue

Diet

One or two tablespoons of special chinchilla food plus a handful of hay twice a day. Once or twice a week, a tiny bit of dried fruit, such as a raisin.

Chapter 1

Chinchilla

Chinchillas are rodents that live in the wild in the Andes Mountains of South America. There they live in burrows, usually in large groups called colonies.

Special Needs

A chinchilla needs a very large cage, at least 6 feet long, 6 feet wide, and 3 feet tall. Chinchillas like toys they can chew, such as wooden blocks. When handling a chinchilla, hold the base of the tail (close to the body) with one hand, while you carry the animal on your other arm, close to your body.

General Behavior

Chinchillas:

1. are active, especially at night.
2. are easily frightened.
3. will allow humans to pick them up but do not always want to be held.
4. can jump very high—probably higher than your head!
5. clean their fur by rolling and digging in dust. This is called a dust bath.

◀ Chinchillas take dust baths to stay clean. You can get special "dust" from a pet store or your vet's office.

Degus burrow, burrow, and then burrow some more!

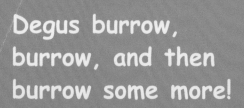

Diet

A tablespoon of degu pellets every day (ask your vet—some can also eat a mixture of chinchilla and guinea pig pellets). Also hay and fresh, raw vegetables, such as sweet potatoes, carrots, and broccoli.

Chapter 2

Degu

Degus (DAY-goos) are rodents. In the wild, they live in South America. They can live in different habitats, from woods by the ocean to rocky mountains. Wherever they live, they like to burrow.

Special Needs

A degu becomes unhealthy if it lives alone (if it was a person you would say it was "depressed"). You must get at least two. They should be of the same sex, because a male and female degu will produce large numbers of babies.

General Behavior

Degus:

1. are active during the day.
2. burrow, burrow, and then burrow some more!
3. are happiest living in a group.
4. communicate using a variety of sounds.
5. chew everything!
6. want to climb all the time.

◀ Degus love to chew as much as they love to burrow. Because of this, their toys should be wood instead of plastic.

Ferrets will chase other animals, including other ferrets.

Appearance

- Long, thin body measuring 13 to 16 inches
- Long, furry tail
- Round head
- Round black eyes
- Close-set ears
- Many different colors, including white, silver, black, and brown

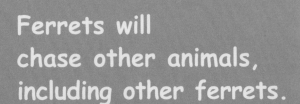

Diet

About one-half cup of ferret food or kitten chow every day (ask your vet what kind), plus cooked meat scraps or eggs as a treat.

Chapter 3

Ferret

The ferrets adopted as pets are related to a wild animal called the polecat. Ferrets have been kept as pets for at least a thousand years! It is illegal to own a ferret in some states, so ask an adult to check with the local animal control officer before deciding to have one as a pet.

General Behavior

Ferrets:

1. are often called curious.
2. are very active!
3. will chase other animals, including other ferrets.
4. will carry off small things, such as socks and cat toys.
5. make nests.

Special Needs

Ferrets will come to their owners when they want to be handled. They need very large wire cages to sleep in, but will not be able to stay in their cages 24 hours a day. They must be allowed outside of their cage at least two hours a day. Longer is better!

◀ A ferret needs to spend time outside of its cage. Make sure it has a safe place to roam where you can watch it carefully.

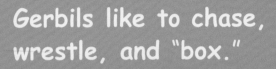
Gerbils like to chase, wrestle, and "box."

Appearance

- Small in size, with a 4-inch-long body
- A long tail that adds another 4 inches to the length
- Round body
- Fluffy fur
- Round face with very large eyes
- Red, brown, or gray in color, with a white belly

Chapter 4

Gerbil

In the wild, gerbils live in dry places in Asia and Africa. These small rodents collect and store food for the winter.

Special Needs

Gerbils can live in a wire cage or terrarium with a lot of bedding at the bottom. They need a lot of exercise equipment, such as tunnels and wheels. Never grab a gerbil by the tip of its tail because its fur, or the tip of the tail itself, might come off, and not grow back. Gerbils need to spend time with other gerbils. They also need to have plenty of things to chew.

General Behavior

Gerbils:
1. have been called curious and friendly.
2. are happiest living in pairs. They should be the same sex, and grow up together from the time they are young.
3. like to chase, wrestle, and "box."
4. groom one another.
5. run very fast through tunnels for exercise.

Diet

Special rodent chow (can come as pellets, which are fed a tablespoon or two at a time, or in a block), plus a few nuts or seeds every day.

◀ Gerbils love burrowing into their bedding. They also love racing through tunnels.

Guinea pigs are active both day and night.

Diet
Hay and greens, such as spinach, kale, or collard greens, plus a tablespoon or two a day of special guinea pig pellets, which have vitamin C.

Chapter 5

Guinea Pig

Guinea pigs no longer live in the wild, but long ago they were found in the Andes Mountains of South America. They have been popular pets in Europe and the United States since the early 1900s.

Special Needs

Be careful when you pick up a guinea pig, because it will squirm. This makes them easy to drop. They need to be allowed to exercise outside of their cage for an hour or two every day. You should do this in a small room that can be closed off.

General Behavior

Guinea pigs:
1. are social animals, so they are happiest living with other guinea pigs of the same sex.
2. are active both day and night.
3. need a lot of activity.
4. can stand on their hind legs.
5. will climb.

◀ Guinea pigs like a regular schedule. They should be fed the same food at the same time every day.

Hamsters sometimes carry food off in their cheeks and bury it.

Appearance

- About the length of your hand—6 to 7 inches. There are dwarf hamsters that are just 3 or 4 inches long!
- Large cheek pouches, used for storing food
- Fluffy fur
- A wide range of colors, including beige, red, rust, and deep brown

Chapter 6

Hamster

In the wild, hamsters live in the Middle East, Africa, and Europe. They are desert creatures that live in burrows. Unlike many other types of small mammals they live alone instead of in groups.

Special Needs

Hamsters can live in a wire cage or glass terrarium. They need to be able to run fast so it is a good idea to buy them an exercise wheel. They will need things to chew. If you are very patient, your hamster may eventually like being picked up.

◀ To help it exercise, give your hamster a large, solid wheel to run in.

General Behavior

Hamsters:

1. are most active at night.
2. love to exercise, climb, and crawl through tunnels.
3. sometimes carry food in their cheeks and bury it.
4. will build themselves a nest (you can give them toilet paper to make it out of).
5. would rather live alone. They can be happy, though, if they are raised with another hamster of the same sex from the time they are young.

Diet

Special hamster chow (you can buy this as pellets, given a tablespoon at a time, or in a block), plus a few nuts or seeds per day.

Hedgehogs grunt, snuffle, and squeal.

Appearance

- Usually 6 inches in length
- Round body
- Short, prickly spines on back
- Furry white belly
- Pointed face
- Upright ears
- Many different colors, including brown, cinnamon, and salt-and-pepper (a mix of black and white)

Chapter 7

Hedgehog

In the wild, hedgehogs live in Africa, Europe, and Asia. If threatened, a hedgehog will roll its body into a ball to protect itself. Since it is illegal to own a hedgehog in some states, ask an adult to check with the local animal control officer before you decide to have one as a pet.

Diet

You will need to discuss this with your vet. In the wild, they eat mostly insects. As pets, some do well eating cat food plus live insects. Sometimes special hedgehog food can also be found.

General Behavior

Hedgehogs:

1. are active mostly at night.
2. like to burrow.
3. sniff everything.
4. grunt, snuffle, and squeal.
5. roll into a ball when they are frightened.

Special Needs

In their home, hedgehogs need an exercise wheel, a hiding place, and deep bedding to allow them to burrow. It will take a long time, but after awhile your hedgehog will let you pick it up. These are fragile creatures that sometimes bite, so they should be handled very carefully.

◄ Hedgehogs look a lot like porcupines, but actually are not related to them.

Mice are happiest when they live in a group.

Appearance

- Small in size, with a body just 2 to 3 inches long
- Hairless tail that can be 3 or 4 inches long
- Pointed face with a pink nose and whiskers
- Beady, black eyes (if the mouse is white, the eyes might be pink)
- Round, pink ears
- White, gray, brown, or black in color

Diet

Special rodent food (this can come as pellets, given by the tablespoon, or in a block), plus a few nuts or seeds per day.

Chapter 8

Mouse

Mice are found just about everywhere in the world. Wild mice live in people's houses and barns, and in fields and forests. They are also popular as pets. But do not be tempted to make a wild mouse a pet. A wild mouse will not be happy locked up in a cage.

General Behavior

Mice:

1. are active both day and night.
2. rarely sit still for more than a minute.
3. like to burrow and climb.
4. are happiest when they live in a group.

Special Needs

Mice need deep bedding in their cage. They will be healthiest if they have at least one other mouse to live with. Both of your mice should be the same sex. You should give your mice an exercise wheel or ball for running. When you pick up a mouse you should not pick it up by its tail. Instead, scoop up its body and then gently hold the tail.

◀ Pet mice are always active and on the go. Burrowing and climbing are their favorite activities.

Rabbits thump their back feet when they sense danger.

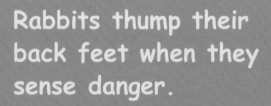

Appearance

- Large in size, measuring up to 20 inches in length
- Round body
- Strong legs
- Short, fluffy tail
- Long, sometimes floppy ears
- Some are long-haired, others short-haired
- Colors include white, many shades of brown, and black. Some rabbits are spotted.

Diet

Rabbit pellets, plus high-fiber foods including hay and dark leafy greens such as spinach, kale, or collard greens. Rabbits should not eat iceberg or red or green leaf lettuce because it contains too much water and will make them sick.

Chapter 9

Rabbit

Rabbits live in burrows in the wild. They are found in many parts of the world. Wild rabbits are shy and avoid humans. You should never try to take in a wild rabbit and raise it.

General Behavior

Rabbits:

1. have been called intelligent creatures.
2. are quiet.
3. like to move around. They hop instead of run.
4. like to chew.
5. thump their back feet when they sense danger.

Special Needs

Rabbits need a very large cage, plus a second place where they can move around freely. They need a hiding and nesting place in their cage, a litter box if they are allowed to roam the house, and plenty of things to chew. Rabbits can be easily trained to use a litter box. Make sure to have your rabbit spayed (if it is a female) or neutered (if it is a male). These are operations that will prevent your rabbits from producing babies. Rabbits that have been spayed or neutered are healthier and make much better pets.

◄ Many pet rabbits spend their time outdoors in a cage. Those that go indoors can easily be trained to use a litter box!

Rats are most active at night.

- Look very much like mice, but bigger, with a body that is 9 to 11 inches long
- Long, hairless tail, 6 or 7 inches long
- Short hair
- Beady eyes
- Rounded ears
- White, gray, brown, or black in color

Diet

One or two tablespoons of special rodent food, plus a few nuts or seeds per day.

Chapter 10

Rat

In the wild, rats are found on every continent except Antarctica. They live almost everywhere humans live. Some wild rats can carry harmful diseases. Pet rats, however, are safe.

Special Needs

Rats are very social and like to live with other rats, so you should try to buy two of the same sex. They also need tunnels or an exercise wheel, and wood shavings to burrow in.

General Behavior

Rats:

1. are most active at night.
2. are very social creatures.
3. have been described as intelligent and playful.
4. sleep in nests.
5. can be trained to use a litter box in their cage.

Rats are social animals and are happiest when living with other rats.

Getting to Know Your New Pet

Getting a new pet is exciting, and small mammals are some of the most fun pets around. One way you can make sure the fun starts right away is to buy your pet's home even before you buy your pet. Set up the cage and hang the water bottle. Add the bedding and a tunnel or box or exercise wheel—or all three!

Once you come home with your new pet, put it in its cage. Now just sit back

Give your pet plenty of time to adjust to its new home. After a while, it may come to you for food, or just to be friendly.

and watch! Do not be tempted to move things around in the cage too much or to try to pick up your pet. It will need time to adjust to its new home.

Show your other family members your pet. Take time to explain to little brothers or sisters that these animals are fragile and easily frightened. They should not make loud noises around your pet or put their fingers in the cage.

In just a day or two, you should take your new pet to the vet for a checkup. Before you go, make a list of questions to ask the vet. One important question is about any medical problems your pet is at risk for. The vet might mention overeating, skin problems, or problems with the teeth.

Also within the first day or so, you should figure out a routine. Plan when you will feed your pet and change its water every day. Choose one day a week to clean its cage. You will also need to think in advance about who will take care of your pet if you go away overnight.

Over time, you will want to get new exercise equipment for your pet so it stays interested and active. You will find it interesting, too, to see your pet figure out how to use a new tunnel or ball.

Soon after you bring your new pet home, take it to the vet for a checkup.

It can take some time for a small mammal to get used to you, so be patient! If you give your pet time to adjust, it will probably come to like having you around and maybe even let you pick it up.

Having a small mammal as a pet will change your life in two important ways. First of all, you will have a big, new responsibility. At the same time, you will be rewarded by having a pet that is always fun to watch.

Glossary

burrow—To dig, especially to make a tunnel or nest, which is also called a burrow.

dust bath—A method some animals use to keep clean. In the wild, they roll in dust. Pets can roll in a special powder.

exotic—Rare or unusual.

habitat—An animal's home.

mammal—A warm-blooded animal that is covered in fur and makes milk to feed its babies.

neutered—When male animals have the organs removed that help them produce babies.

pellets—A type of animal food.

rodent—A small, gnawing (chewing) animal, such as a mouse or guinea pig.

spayed—When female animals have the organs removed that help them produce babies.

terrarium—A box made of glass that can be a habitat for animals.

veterinarian (vet)—A doctor who takes care of animals.

Further Reading

Bjorkland, Ruth. *Rabbits*. Tarrytown, N.Y.: Benchmark Books, 2007.

Fox, Sue. *Gerbils*. Neptune City, N.J.: TFH Publications, 2007.

Jeffrey, Laura S. *Hamsters, Gerbils, Guinea Pigs, Rabbits, Ferrets, Mice, and Rats: How to Choose and Care for a Small Mammal.* Berkeley Heights, N.J.: Enslow, 2004.

McNichols, June. *Ferrets*. Chicago: Heinemann Library, 2003.

Siino, Betsy Sikora. *Hamster: Your Happy Healthy Pet.* Hoboken, N.J.: Howell Book House, 2006.

Internet Addresses

American Humane Association
http://www.americanhumane.org

ASPCA Animaland
http://www.animaland.org

House Rabbit Society
http://www.rabbit.org

Index